MIGUEL MAÑARA

The Library of the Christian Spirit

MIGUEL MAÑARA

by Oscar Vladislas Milosz

With a commentary by
Luigi Giussani

HAB
HUMAN ADVENTURE BOOKS
TAMPA

Miguel Mañara
By Oscar Vladislas Milosz

Translated 1985 from the French by Edo Morlin-Visconti
Substantial Edit 2017 by Melissa Massy

Translation and introduction to the play used by kind
permission of the translator.

Commentary by Luigi Giussani property of The
Fraternity of Communion and Liberation. Used with
permission.

Original title:
Miguel Mañara. Mystère en six tableaux (1913)
In the Public Domain

CONTENTS

LUIGI GIUSSANI

Commentary on
MIGUEL MAÑARA

*From a reading of the play with a group of
university students in January, 1980.*

I would like to highlight some selections from one of the texts that helped to build the history of the Fraternity of Communion and Liberation. Along with Paul Claudel's play *The Tidings Brought to Mary,* Oscar Milosz's play *Miguel Mañara* is so central to the movement that our members practically memorized the play line by line.

Miguel Mañara is the real Don Giovanni. Miguel was an historical figure in the mid-sixteen hundreds. He is the original Spanish Don Giovanni who gave rise to all the subsequent "Don Giovanni" characters. He is rich in all senses; in all the talents and possibilities imaginable. Therefore, Miguel is hopelessly arrogant. Everything is due to him, and everything must serve his pleasure and his opinion. Violence, in the most subtle and masked sense, is the law of his life. The knights of the king's court respect him as "the best" even though he is at least half their age.

The play opens with a party given in Miguel's honor. The drunk guests provoke Miguel to recount all his adventures with women of any type and social class. Miguel's answers produce admiration in the guests who cry out: "Glory to Mañara, glory to Mañara in the depths of hell!" To this Miguel replies:

I am pleased to see, sirs, that you all love me a lot, and I am deeply moved by the heartfelt wish you express of seeing my flesh and my spirit burning alive in a new flame, very far from here. I swear before you on my honor and on the head of the Bishop of Rome that your hell does not exist, and has never burned except in the mind of a mad Messiah or an evil monk.

But we know that in God's empty space there are worlds illumined by a joy warmer than ours, unexplored and wonderful lands that are very, very far from this one. So, go ahead and choose one of these far and delightful planets, and send me there, this very night, through the grave's greedy door. For time passes slowly, sirs, terribly slowly, and I am strangely tired of this bitch of a life. Not to reach God is certainly a tiny thing, but to lose Satan is a great sorrow and a huge bore, by my faith!

I have drawn Love into pleasure, into the mud, and into death; I have been a traitor, a blasphemer, an executioner; I have done all that a poor devil of a man can do, and look! I have lost Satan. I eat the bitter herb of the rock of boredom; I have served Venus in anger, in malice, and finally in disgust. Today I would yawn as I twisted her neck. And it is not vanity speaking through my mouth. I do not pose as an insensitive executioner.

I've suffered; I've suffered much. Anguish has winked his eye at me; jealousy has whispered into my ear, pity has grabbed me by the throat. Really, these were the least deceptive among my pleasures.

So! My confession takes you by surprise; I hear some of you laughing. Know then that there is no one who ever committed a truly shameful action who did not cry over his victim. Certainly, in my young years, I too sought, just as you do, the miserable joy, the restless stranger who gives you her life without telling you her name. But the desire was soon born in me to pursue what you'll never know: a love immense, dark and sweet. More than once I thought I had caught it, but it was only a ghostly flame. I'd embrace it, and with an oath I'd promise it eternal tenderness. But the flame would only burn my lips and cover my head with my own ashes. When I opened my eyes again, there was only the horrible day of loneliness. All that existed was a long, endless day of loneliness that held nothing in its hands but a poor, poor sweet heart, as light as a sparrow in winter. And one evening, the vile-eyed and low-browed lust came to sit on my bed, and looked at me in silence, as if looking at a dead man.

Do you know what I need, sirs? A new beauty, a new sorrow, a new love that I'll soon be fed up with! Why? To taste better the wine of a new evil, a new life, and gain an infinity of new lives. That's what I need, sirs, nothing else.

Ah, how do I fill up this emptiness in life? What can I do? For the desire is always there, stronger and madder than ever. It's like a fire in the sea that blasts its flame into the deep universal black emptiness.

It is a desire to embrace the infinite possibilities. Ah sirs, what are we doing here? What do we gain? Ah, how short is this life according to science! Too short also in supply of weapons; why this poor world wouldn't even have enough to satisfy the appetites of a lord like me. And as far as good works are concerned, you know that men are troublesome dogs; they are a stinking brood of rats! Certainly, you know too that a King is a very poor thing once God has gone away.

There is no difference between Miguel's cry of frustration with desire and the song sung by the Roundelay in Andre Gide's play *The Fruits of the Earth (Middlesex, England: Penguin Books Ltd, 1970), 75-76.*

Desire, I dragged you with me along the high roads; I have denied you in the fields; I have sated you with drink in the big towns — sated you without quenching your thirst; I have bathed you in moonlit nights; I have taken you with me wherever I went; I have cradled you on the waves; I have lulled you to sleep on the high seas... Desire! Desire! What more can I do for you? What more do you want? Will you never weary?

Among those present, Don Fernando is the only wise and well-balanced man. He is the eldest in the group and a friend of Miguel's father. Don Fernando intuits that his friend's son is going through a horrible and desperate moment in his life. Don Fernando's remedy is to imaging Miguel in a friend's house where there lives only one daughter, Girolama. She is a very young, an intelligent, beautiful, direct, and serene woman.

In the second scene, the first in-depth dialogue between Miguel and Girolama reveals that Girolama is a presence that produces a change in Miguel. "Why", says Miguel, "have I never realized before that I have a good soul?" Girolama's presence, in fact, makes Miguel's awareness of himself possible. Do we also feel this deep, calm, free, and pure adventure of love in our own lives?

The dialogue between Miguel and Girolama is so intense and great that it should be read word by word because it is the event that solidifies Miguel's transformation.

DON MIGUEL

You love flowers, Girolama? And I don't see them in your hair or on your person.

GIROLAMA

It is because I love flowers that I do not like girls who adorn themselves with them, as with silk or lace or colourful feathers. I never put flowers in my hair as it's beautiful enough, thank God! Flowers are beautiful living beings that we must let live and breathe the air of the sun and of the moon. I never pick flowers. We can very well love, in this world where we are, without wanting immediately to kill the one we love, or to imprison it behind glass, or, as people do with birds, to lock them up in a cage in which water no longer tastes like water and summer seeds no longer taste like seeds.

DON MIGUEL

So, everything is honey, dew, and balm of sweetness in you, Girolama? Is there no dark corner in your heart? Do you never get angry?

GIROLAMA

But yes, yes! And even against these flowers, I like so much, because their Latin names are so hard to remember. They have earned me an infinite number of lectures from our abbot, who, instead of contenting himself with being good at geometry, dedicates himself to botany, too, to my great misfortune.

You were telling me awhile ago that my life was sad; I don't agree at all. There is the house, the garden, the daily lesson, and the poor. There are many, a great many poor people in Seville. I have no time to get bored. And then there are books. You see, I am the one who reads to my father. I know almost all our poets, and recently we acquired "The Adventures of the Illustrious Knight of La Mancha." My father and the abbot laughed a lot, and I wanted to cry. How beautiful are the books that make you laugh and cry at the same time!

But maybe I am stretching your patience too long, Don Miguel, and you must be judging me very dull and garrulous. You look a bit surprised at seeing me so happy. Do not reproach me for this peace of mind and heart, for I neglect none of my duties.

DON MIGUEL

I was the one, Girolama, who asked you to tell me the story of your dear life. Oh, sweet life, oh beautiful and sad flower! Do not withdraw your hand; leave it here on my heart. Let the beating of my heart manage to tell you what I don't dare entrust to my voice. I've so many things to tell you! I am so changed from the day we met! It was at the church of Caridad, remember? Around Palm Sunday, before I left for Madrid; and that same evening Don Fernando, your father's old friend, pushed me by the shoulders into this house which I feared, because you knew my life. You knew of my life, as much as can be revealed to a young girl, and it is a lot, I'm afraid. It is too much, Girolama.

GIROLAMA

I spoke to Don Fernando. Maybe I should not confess these things to you, but I spoke to Don Fernando about you. I'm no longer a child and I think that nothing is better than beautiful honesty. And Don Fernando spoke to me about you. You know how he is, our old friend Don Fernando: a bit of a teaser, but a good fellow. He told me a joke (he knew me as a baby), then suddenly he changed his tone, and even his expression. And he spoke to me about you.

DON MIGUEL

Alas, Girolama! There is no remedy to this sadness of the heart! What's done is done. Because life is like that. What's done is done.

GIROLAMA

I don't agree in the least. I see nothing so terrible in this. I know you are a bad lot, who has made many ladies cry, and beautiful ones, too. But all these women knew they were doing wrong in loving you, and even in allowing you to love them. For you have given none of them the oath, the great oath that binds for eternity, Don Miguel. You had given none of them the ring, the ring that unites soul to soul forever, Don Miguel. Ah, they knew very well what they were doing, all of them, yes, all of them!

DON MIGUEL

Silence! Your voice frightens me, Girolama! It is as if a summer-beam suddenly penetrates a place protected by the wings of night, full of crawling shapes. A night full of things dreamt of by the sickness of darkness. One day I saw a Sister of Mercy pushing her way all alone into the cell of those condemned to death. This is how your voice advances, Girolama, into my evil heart.

GIROLAMA

It is because you take me for a stupid little girl; it is because you don't know me well, Don Miguel. And it is because I am small and weak. I am sure you feel a great compassion for me, fearing you could break my wing or my little paw. But I give you leave to speak to me freely. I am not afraid of you.

Something in my heart tells me I'm your sister. I am not afraid of your eyes. No, Miguel, your look does not frighten me. I know well that at times, you are watching me as one watches a small animal he wants to catch, and it always makes me laugh when I think of it. You say woman is weak; all men say it, I think, for my father says it, and the abbot, and Don Fernando. And books say so, too. It's a fact, woman is weak. But like the bird in the air and the small mouse in the field: just wanting to catch it does not mean it is caught. And women know very well what they are doing. Wake up, Don Miguel. Women don't let themselves be taken except when God is no longer in their heart, and then it's no longer worth while taking them. I know well what I say and do, otherwise, would I have come here, alone? I took great interest in letting you know me, Don Miguel. For you, I know you. Three months have passed since the day we met at Caridad, Don Miguel; and you certainly are not now what you were then.

DON MIGUEL

Yes, Girolama, what you say is true; I am not what I was. I see better; yet I was not blind. Perhaps it was the light that was missing. The exterior light is a small thing; it is not the one that enlightens our life. You have lit a lamp in my heart. Here I am, like the sick man who falls asleep in darkness with the embers of fever on his forehead and the ice of desertion in his heart. A sick man who suddenly wakes up in a beautiful room in which everything is immersed in the discreet music of light; and he sees the friend he has mourned for many years...the friend who is full of happy noises to feast the man who was saved from the flood of darkness! Behold what a place of peace you've changed my heart into, Girolama! My sweetest sister! For, a while ago you said you were my sister, didn't you?

GIROLAMA

You are the man saved from the flood of darkness! You are weak, pale, and still stupefied; it is well and necessary that a sister should think for you, speak for you, support you on the way, and pray to God for you. Aren't you the man saved from the bitter water? Then, certainly, I am your sister.

DON MIGUEL

But if you truly are my sweet sister, Girolama, precisely my... No, I cannot say it, my voice is no longer my voice, my heart is no longer my heart, my life is no longer my life... Girolama, give me your weak hand, your dearest hand of a friend, of a sister, of a holy spouse!

GIROLAMA

Are you talking to a young girl or to a woman? Beware, for heaven is listening, Don Miguel.

DON MIGUEL

I am talking to a woman under the shining sky of my joy, under the heavens suspended above our heads like a perfumed vault. I am talking to you, Girolama! You who are very great, so very great as to make me afraid? What have I done with my life? What have I done with my heart? Why didn't I learn earlier that I have a good soul? Will you forgive me?

GIROLAMA

I will have to forgive you. Get up.

DON MIGUEL

What about your hand?

GIROLAMA

I will have to give it to you.

DON MIGUEL

What about your heart? Are you going to refuse it to my joy? Tell me, what about your heart?

GIROLAMA

My heart is no longer mine.

DON MIGUEL

And your great purity, and your own holiness, will you entrust them to me, for as long as time, for as long as life lasts?

GIROLAMA

For as long as eternity.

DON MIGUEL

And do you love me? Do you love me with a devoted love before men?

GIROLAMA

Before God.

The play does not back away from the truth of this needed Presence of one to the other.

As Miguel says:

Alas, Girolama! There is no remedy to this sadness of the heart! What's done is done. Because life is like that. What's done is done.

And Girolama opposes this: "*I don't agree in the least.*"

There is a Presence through which the past, with all it's evil, becomes a life, a different life; it becomes the truth of one's own existence unknown until that moment.

It is a rebirth, as Miguel says: "Because I never realized that I had a good soul."

It's like a recovery of the world, like someone who exits the night for the first time and sees, finally sees the reality of the world. An embrace of everything becomes possible: an embrace of what was distant, what was lost, of what was near but unseen. It is an embrace of family, and dogs.

Girolama is a sign to Miguel. She is a presence that makes him raise up in an universal embrace. These factors belong to the structure of our life. In varying degrees, each of us has caught a glimpse of the nearness of this transformative Presence. If we are here it is because of this kind of encounter. However distant an Echo it might have been, this is the kind of event that engages me.

Indeed, what is the purpose of being here for each other if not for this companionship that cherishes and cares for us like an intention of the heart? What are we doing here? What do each of you mean for the other? When one day you find yourselves, man and woman together, and it is to your advantage to continue on together, will it be for a solely human attachment? An attachment yet without echoes, perspectives, or voice? What are you for her, and you, what is she for you? You must aspire to freely allow your heart to journey towards the idea. If you choose not to walk toward this different life, then what are you if not a lump which only responds to the other's spontaneous instinct, or state of the soul?

At a certain point Girolama explains the consequences of choosing something other than a loving companionship.

We can very well love, in this world where we are, without wanting immediately to kill the one we love, or to imprison it behind glass, or, as people do with birds, to lock them up in a cage in which water no longer tastes like water and summer seeds no longer taste like seeds.

Girolama's way of loving is a way that does not desire to grab another in order to possess them or stop their growth. Rather, she explains that if one chooses not to give the other a hand in their journey towards their destiny, one murders and puts an end to them.

After three months of marriage, Girolama unexpectedly dies.

Now Miguel finds himself virtually suspended over a vertiginous abyss within which he no longer has the support of a loving presence. And he cannot go back to the way he was before, because once you have glimpsed certain things, you cannot return to the way it was before. The presence is no longer there, but the presentiment of his destiny that the presence gave him remains. He can no longer deny that truth of the world he has learned; that perspective on his journey, that destiny of his life. But now that Girolama is gone, where can that presence now be found? A desperate seeker of support, companionship, and a loving presence, Miguel knocks at the door of the Convent.

The fourth scene begins with dialogue between Miguel and the Abbot, in whose character is revealed another form of the same companionship Miguel had with Girolama. The core of the dialogue in this scene lies in the intensely passionate unveiling of what prayer is. Here is the possibility of companionship that, in any moment and condition of life whatsoever, makes man sense the presence that cannot fail. This possibility reveals to man all the precariousness and limits of a human presence. The frail human companionship is a sign that points to God, the eternal Presence with a capital P.

The characters of Girolama and the abbot are human signs for Miguel of that eternal companionship that never fails. Regardless of whether the companion is as frail as Girolama or as powerful as the abbot, neither human presence can accompany Miguel in every step of his journey. However, even the limited human companionship gives Miguel a sense of the eternal Presence and this becomes a part of him that no longer desires to withdraw or vanish. To embrace that presence, Don Miguel must make his confession. Miguel cries out in despair over himself and his life. He is dominated by shame for his evil. The presence of Girolama and then her absence makes all the vomit of his past life return.

THE ABBOT

...Come on, come on, do not cry, my son. No! He does not want to smile, my begging monk. I cannot get a smile out of him! Don't you understand then, my son? The fact is you are thinking of things that are no more and that never were, my son.

But is it necessary to remind you that you have come, that you are here, that all is well? What is there in that head of his, Lord?

23

DON MIGUEL

How can you read my heart in this way, Father? You did not even give me time to open it all to you. How do you read my heart, a closed book, like this, Father?

THE ABBOT

Get up. You are being strange. And stop embracing my knees. Can't you keep quiet? I'll have your cell prepared. Do you hear me? I want to have you very close. Your nights will be very long, deserted, and hard. Just wait a bit and see what comes to a man dressed in vanity! You are going to find out what prayer is all about. You are going to know how a man prays, alone, at night, between four walls made of eternity. Ah, prayer is not your fountains of tears under the moon! Say your prayers among four walls that pretend to be deaf. Speak your litanies virgin of thought and naked of reason as long as a shadow of love escapes. I want to have you very close. But you will never call for me. Understand? You will only say to yourself, "the Father is there, behind these walls that never dream. The Father is there, he is old, and he sleeps on his three planks. And I am all alone with the heart of stone, and I breathe my prayers into the ear of stone." For you men dressed in colors say that walls have ears for your plots and your blasphemies. But here, life is a thing very different from a smile in a woman's lipstick or a tear fallen on glass. Here the stones are full of a patience that waits and a waiting that listens.

DON MIGUEL

*Dark cell! Image of my heart! Lovable mortifications!
Silence of catacombs! How I love you already!*

THE ABBOT

*Love and haste do not agree, Mañara. It is by patience
that love is measured. This is the pace of love: a pace
both regular and sure. The pace of love that walks
between two jasmine hedges, arm in arm with a girl,
or alone between two rows of tombs. Patience. You
have not come here, sir, to be tortured. Life is long here.
Infancy and education are necessary, along with youth,
and teaching. Only then will you develop a maturity
curious about the right weight of things, and a slow old
age in love with the grave. With what prudence must we
move then! For the burning hair-shirt has no love for
the violence that quenches the blood's itching. So, you
must keep very still in a short, narrow coffin when you
desire to sleep an hour or two. For in prayer, sleep is as
empty and as deep as the instant.*

*To let your own blood is something sweetly fiendish;
and sleeplessness consumes the heart. Now, life is long
here, you understand. And too exasperated a hunger
is a temptation. You must chew the foul grass and
the lukewarm root like an animal which has before it
beautiful meadows and long, long hours of summer.*

*And you must talk to Eternity with precious and clear
syllables even at night, when its love grabs you by the
throat like a murderer.*

Know too that it is an excellent thing to remain faithful to the word that was ordered, a dam of granite for the bitter waters of your love! For it is necessary that prayer be a fast before it is a banquet, and nakedness of heart before it is a mantle of heaven buzzing with worlds. Perhaps a day will come when God allows you to enter brutally, like an axe, into the flesh of the tree. A day will come when you fall madly like a stone into the night of the water, and to slip, singing like fire, into the heart of metal.

...

My dear child, all this may well come one day, when the snake has changed his skin. But one must start from the beginning: this is essential.

When the perception of God and Christ have become quite clear in the plant, and in the tree, and in the water, when the mystery that is the core of the plant, of the water, and of metal, of the earth and sky, then the heart is no longer separated. When the heart is no longer separated, as if the veil had fallen, then you see the outline traced by the body behind the veil.

To bite the stone and to bark, "Lord, Lord, Lord!" is to weep and serve a heartless woman. You must leave this to the betrayed who sigh for one night, or six months, or ten years.

Life is long here.

You will beware therefore of inventing prayers. You will sing humbly with the book of the poor in spirit. And you will wait.

From the last nightly spark of your madness, the first dawn will spring up!

The crater of the heart cries and thunders and the black vomit will leave the cloud, falling back in grey famine on the field and the vineyard. A prayer that devastates passion is like that. But when the heart has fallen asleep in the balm of the years, when the flesh has died and the blood has gone pale, you will no longer speak to God of yourself. When the marrow has gone dry, and when love and sorrow are past, you will no longer speak to God of yourself. When love, sorrow, and hatred have become ghosts that the sword penetrates as it does water, and when the lip hits nothing more than its own wound, as in molten glass, it is then that you speak to God no longer of yourself and of your own miserable unhappiness, but of man. It is then you will speak to God of the breaking waves of sea foam, of the sand, of the wind, and of the rain! Do you know which saint said, "Behold brother wind and sister rain?"

O my son, if you knew what things man can tell God when man's flesh becomes a cry, the cry of God worshiping Himself!

You do not have the face of a man who is listening, Miguel. You are thinking too much of your own sorrow. Why do you seek sorrow? Why are you afraid of losing what has managed to find you? Penance is not sorrow. It is love.

Now the abbot leaves the scene and Miguel is alone. After a long life in the convent contemplating these things, Miguel's final soliloquy begins.

DON MIGUEL

Look at the moon, look at the earth, look at man so weak and at his great sorrow. And yet, despite all these things that are, I dare not say that You are.

Who am I, then, that I should dare say that You are? I am not sure, I have no right to be sure of anything apart from one: of my love, of my love, of my blind love for You. Nothing is pure, except my love for You. Nothing is great, except my love for You. The dream has vanished; the passion has run away; the remembrance was canceled. Love has remained. Nothing is sincere, except my love for You. Nothing is real, except my love for You. Nothing is immortal, except my love for You.

For I am nothing but one dead man among the dead whom I have loved, I am nothing but a name that fills the mouth of the living with sand. What's left is Love. Ah, Beauty! The sad, poor Beauty! But I want to praise Beauty, for it is from Beauty that Sorrow is born. The beloved of the Beloved. Your great love burns my heart. Your great love is my sole certainty. O tears! O hunger for eternity! O joy! Alas! Forgive! Alas! Love me!

There are great men and small men, there are mature men and there are children, but the story line of humanity applies to every heart. We are children, but we are called for this journey where nothing is lost, nothing is forgotten, and, above all, nothing is renounced. Rather, everything is regained; everything is finally found. From the appearance of Beauty, the Sadness that redeems it comes about, and finally, Love comes about. The verb "to love" has no chance whatsoever of being ambiguous. Love affirms, with the wonder of all one's being, the presence of the Other, and of Destiny. This presence of Destiny, this sign, is the sky and the earth and everything that happens. My goodness, my sorrow, and my evil become worthy of love. Everything is new. "Everything is new," says Saint Paul. Behold, the old has passed away; it no longer exists. We are children once again. This is the path we are called to before everything. There's nothing to forget or renounce; there's no mutilation. There is only a resurrection.

We are not afraid, even if what we see is mortification. What is mortification? It is contained within the sentiment expressed by the relatives of Christ Jesus' in the Gospel: "Come home, you're mad." Although everything evidently corresponds to the passionate and indisputable yearning in our heart for God, we're dealing with an announcement that is totally foreign to everyday speech. Yet we are called to become great like Christ.

Let us pray to the Lord, pray to Him who has given us Being, the Father, He who is our destiny, original consistency of our life and our end; let us pray to He through whom we are born in every instant, that He make of our lives such a mature fruit, that He make us so great, that He make us run the whole length of the journey. Let us pray, let us ask God.

Let us remember that prayer is asking Christ and that's it. Because within that there is father, mother, brother, sister, husband, wife, boyfriend, girlfriend, friend, companion, man, sky, and earth. It's there within. This, indeed, is the formula for truth: *God, all in all*. It's the formula of existence towards the explosion of that truth: *Christ, everything in everyone*. The truth that the Mystery of our companionship is the fragile and precarious but true sign of his Presence. Let us pray to God.

MIGUEL MAÑARA

Oscar V. Milosz

MIGUEL MAÑARA

Oscar V. Milosz
Introduction

THE AUTHOR

Oscar Vladislas Milosz was born in Lithuania in 1877, and died in Fontainebleau, France, in 1939.

His father, Vladislas Milosz, married Marie Rosalie Rosenthale, a Jewess, and kept her away from any social life because Jews were the objects of spite in the Lithuanian milieu. During his early years, the poet suffered because his mother was always full of resentment towards her husband and she even mistreated her child.

In 1889, the family moved to Paris, and the father sent Milosz to a French high school. From this moment, Milosz's heart was divided. Milosz had a strong, nostalgic affection for his Country of origin, Lithuania, and for its Catholic culture. However, he also loved the charm of the French language and the secular education he received at school. Although Milosz wrote his poetry and dramas in French, many of his publications draw from remembrances of the cold forests and wintry songs of his beloved Lithuania.

After high school, starting in 1899, Milosz wrote and published various books of poetry. In 1910 he wrote a novel called, Amorous Initiation: A Novel of Sacred and Profane Love (Rochester: Inner Traditions, 1st English edition, 1993). In this novel Milosz shows signs of his conversion when he affirms that "He who truly loves, loves God". From 1911 to 1915, Milosz wrote most of his outstanding dramas including Miguel Mañara, Saul of Tarsus, and Mephiboseth.

In 1918 when Lithuania became an independent Republic, Milosz obtained citizenship and immediately joined the Diplomatic Service, representing his country in France as Charge d'Affaires. Milosz resigned from the Service in1925 but remained attached to the Embassy until 1938 when he abandoned all diplomatic activity. This was just one year before his death.

During his years as a diplomat, Milosz devoted his energy to making the culture and tradition of Lithuania known to the French public and to Western Europe in general. He also wrote philosophical and mystical works. In 1938, Milosz published his last work called La Clef de l'Apocalypse (The Key to the Apocalypse; Paris, Firmin-Didot, 1938). This essay presents his studies on the interpretation of the Bible.

MIGUEL MAÑARA

This drama is defined by the author as a "Mystery in Six Flashes." Each "Flash" is a circumscribed scene and contains a story within the story. The central theme of each flash depicts man having a unique, unrepeatable encounter with the Mystery of God.

Miguel Mañara tells the conversion story of a Spanish nobleman in the 17th century. Don Miguel Mañara journeys from the career of an exceptional womanizer to the highest degree of holiness.

The first flash shows how bored a man can become in a life dedicated to sin, despite the unequaled success his peers accord him. We could describe this flash as the first insurgence of the religious sense in a person. There always comes a point, the author implies, where long-repressed fundamental questions can no longer be dodged.

The second flash presents the story of an encounter that begins to dissolve Miguel's womanizing tendencies. Don Miguel is introduced to a young girl, Girolama, who intrigues him because she is different from all the others he has met before. The veteran womanizer is captured by her gentle firmness and by her deep attachment to prayer. Miguel realizes he cannot have the kind of relationship he is used to. In other words, Miguel cannot use and dispose of Girolama. Fascinated by her humanity, so different and fresh, Miguel learns to pray again, and eventually asks her to marry him in Church.

Three months after the wedding, Girolama dies. In the third flash, the young widower recognizes in his sorrow the way in which God is calling him to a new life; a life on earth containing the seed of eternity.

Miguel seeks refuge and spiritual solace in the convent at Caridad. The fourth flash displays his encounter with the Father Superior, or Abbot. The Abbot receives his confession and invites him to join the Carmelite religious life as his only chance to undergo a real change. The long nights in prayerful penance will enable don Miguel, the

Abbot promises, to fully experience the love of God after a life spent in debauchery and in irreverence to love.

In the fifth flash, the author shows us the visible signs of God's fruits in a man who has really entrusted his life to God. Two religious men talk to each other about Friar Miguel's astonishing conversion. A man who truly is changed by God's love can become an instrument of His loving power: through Miguel, a lame beggar is miraculously healed in the public square.

The sixth flash shows the apotheosis of conversion. Friar Miguel is now a very old friar who dies and is welcomed by the Father in heaven in the way that had been prophesied to him many years before. To those who love God, and who are chosen by Him to enter His Mystery on earth, maturity is indeed the realization of the dreams of youth.

Edo Morlin-Visconti

Dramatis Personae

Don Miguel Mañara Vincentelo De Leca

Don Jaime

Don Fernando

The Abbot of the Convent of Caridad at Seville

Two Religious Men of the same Order

Johannes Mendelez, a Paralysed Beggar

Gorolama Carillo De Mendoza

The Shadow

The Spirits of the Earth

The Spirit of Heaven

Voices from the crowd

FIRST FLASH

The scene opens at Seville, in the year of grace 1656.

The castle of Don Jaime in the countryside of Seville. A banquet in a brightly lit hall. Almost all the guests are already the worse for wine.

Don Jaime, a short plump old man of brutish appearance, is standing on a chair reproaching waiters and valets in a raucous voice.

DON JAIME

By the wounds of Christ! It seems to me that my guest, Don Miguel Vincentelo de Leca, knight of Calatrava, is letting himself die of thirst! God forbid that I should force you, Lenten-faced rogues, to stuff yourselves with black meat or yellow fat, or to drown yourselves in wine. We are, if our Lord Bacchus does not induce me into error, in the holiest of the yearly seasons, between Ash Wednesday and Palm Sunday. So then, rascals, fast, by all the devils, till the Catholic fast pushes through your skin with all its long rotten teeth, that are nothing but your own son-of-a-bitch bones. But, by Mohammed, as my servants you will go on serving as in the ordinary reveling and boozing time; or else I will send you to fast till Judgment Day in the antechamber of Monsignor the Archbishop, that saintly arch-miser. Come on, some wine, some wine! Or else, hell, I am going to swear in such a way that you will all be damned.

Wine is brought.

And then if the Inquisition appears in the doorway, draw your swords, you lazy rascals, draw your swords and ready with the fuses, by the devil! Because...

DON MIGUEL

Sit down, you damned bawler, and stop bragging. Who here does not know your madman's antiphon! Here's one who thinks himself an enemy of Christ, yet, on my honour, would never dare, on a Good Friday, to lay hands on a scullery-maid caught in the dark passage between the cellar and the kitchen.

DON JAMIE

Ah, villain, come here onto my heart! Let me give you a great smacking kiss! You can teach the rest of us! What are we, poor miserable-looking devils, what are we compared to you? But what am I saying, compared with your shadow! You really are what I can call a wicked bastard. Look how handsome he is tonight! Eleanor, Blanche, Lawrence, and you Ines, and Cynthia, and all of you down there, just look at him! Have you ever set your eyes, you bitches, on a nobler forehead, a more beautiful mouth, a more passionate eye? And this silky lace from Venice, this shirt, by Bacchus! This king of shirts! And this sword, and this dress! Tell me, son, how many duchesses have you got on your conscience?

MANY VOICES

Yes, yes! How many seated duchesses? How many duchesses with the right of stool?

DON MIGUEL

Six.

DON JAIME

How many high-ranking marquesses?

DON MIGUEL

Seven, eight, or nine, if my lord Eros does not deceive me.

DON JAIME

And noble and middle-class girls?

DON MIGUEL

Between sixty and a hundred. I don't keep a full list.

DON JAIME

And small-time whores?

DON MIGUEL

There was once one who loved me truly, and died of unfeigned despair.

Short silence.

And she died, sirs, almost at the same time as Sister Magdalene of the Compassion, stolen from Jesus thanks to my attentions.

ALL

Glory to Mañara, glory to Mañara in the lowest of hells!

Tumult of laughter, shouts, tinkling of silver and clinking of glasses.

DON MIGUEL

I am pleased to see, sirs, that you all love me a lot, and I am deeply moved by the heartfelt wish you express of seeing my flesh and my spirit burning alive in a new flame, very far from here. I swear before you on my honor and on the head of the Bishop of Rome that your hell does not exist, and has never burned except in the mind of a mad Messiah or an evil monk.

But we know that in God's empty space there are worlds illumined by a joy warmer than ours, unexplored and wonderful lands that are very, very far from this one. So, go ahead and choose one of these far and delightful planets, and send me there, this very night, through the grave's greedy door. For time passes slowly, sirs, terribly slowly, and I am strangely tired of this bitch of a life. Not to reach God is certainly a tiny thing, but to lose Satan is a great sorrow and a huge bore, by my faith!

I have drawn Love into pleasure, into the mud, and into death; I have been a traitor, a blasphemer, an executioner; I have done all that a poor devil of a man can do, and look! I have lost Satan. I eat the bitter herb of the rock of boredom; I have served Venus in anger, in malice, and finally in disgust. Today I would yawn as I twisted her neck. And it is not vanity speaking through my mouth. I do not pose as an insensitive executioner. I've suffered; I've suffered much. Anguish has winked his eye at me; jealousy has whispered into my ear, pity has grabbed me by the throat. Really, these were the least deceptive among my pleasures.

So! My confession takes you by surprise; I hear some of you laughing. Know then that there is no one who ever committed a truly shameful action who did not cry over his victim. Certainly, in my young years, I too sought, just as you do, the miserable joy, the restless stranger who gives you her life without telling you her name. But the desire was soon born in me to pursue what you'll never know: a love immense, dark and sweet. More than once I thought I had caught it, but it was only a ghostly flame. I'd embrace it, and with an oath I'd promise it eternal tenderness. But the flame would only burn my lips and cover my head with my own ashes. When I opened my eyes again, there was only the horrible day of loneliness. All that existed was a long, endless day of loneliness that held nothing in its hands but a poor, poor sweet heart, as light as a sparrow in winter. And one evening, the vile-eyed and low-browed lust came to sit on my bed, and looked at me in silence, as if looking at a dead man.

Do you know what I need, sirs? A new beauty, a new sorrow, a new love that I'll soon be fed up with! Why? To taste better the wine of a new evil, a new life, and gain an infinity of new lives. That's what I need, sirs, nothing else.

Ah, how do I fill up this emptiness in life? What can I do? For the desire is always there, stronger and madder than ever. It's like a fire in the sea that blasts its flame into the deep universal black emptiness.

It is a desire to embrace the infinite possibilities. Ah sirs, what are we doing here? What do we gain? Ah, how short is this life according to science! Too short also in supply of weapons; why this poor world wouldn't even have enough to satisfy the appetites of a lord like me. And as far as good works are concerned, you know that men are troublesome dogs; they are a stinking brood of rats! Certainly, you know too that a King is a very poor thing once God has gone away.

In a low voice, turning to MIGUEL.

DON FERNANDO

If you see me here despite my white hair, Miguel, it is because I have been keeping an eye on you for a long time. I was the best friend of your father, Don Tomaso Vincentelo de Leca; and I knew your mother, Donna Girolama Anfriano. Your mother was a holy woman. Your father was a worthy man, faithful to God and his King. He died in my arms. Look at me, Miguel. You see I do not lower my eyes and I am no paler than before because I tell you what I must: you are a coward and a criminal.

DON MIGUEL

Are you mad or drunk, Don Fernando, or are you tired of living?

DON FERNANDO

You know I have grown old in very holy battles, and that I will never part from my sword, even in death. I have had four horses killed under me, and I speak to the king face to face without taking off my hat. I could pull your ears, you scoundrel, but I content myself by repeating: you are a coward and a criminal. Whoever mistreats a woman and betrays her is a coward and a criminal. And who ever desires the woman of another man is a vile bastard. And who ever robs the least country girl of the holy treasure of her virginity, and then abandons her to her shame and despair, whoever does this is a dog, and must die like a dog. You are no gentleman, Miguel, you are a dog. Your coat-of-arms is something to be pinned above the door of a brothel. Is it my fault if the smell of your face-powder and of your make-up reminds me of a dog's smell? Tell me, Don Miguel, knight of Calatrava, is it my fault? If your father were alive, I would spit in your face; but your father is dead. He is no longer here to defend the honour of his blood; and your mother is no longer here to dry the cheek of her child and to console him in her arms.

What have we come to? Is this today's chivalry?

Even a Jew in the stench of his ghetto, a Jew faithful to his wife and tender with his little ones, is a thousand times more of a gentleman than yourself! For whom then did we fight, powers of heaven! For whom then did our

King sacrifice his own life, he who could not even love according to his heart, he who went pale and yellow before time in the dust of the State parchments. Alas!

He hides his face between his hands.

A rather long silence, then he continues.

DON FERNANDO

Listen to me, Miguel. You are young. Thirty years old. I don't know if I should laugh or cry! You are blessed with a nasty but powerful reason. Thirty! It's like the smell of grain fields, like the smile of night at the window where a face must appear, sweetly illumined by the heart of a rose.

Miguel! My son! My child! I am a crazy old man! I have talked to you like an old idiot! I have been unjust. When I was young, I liked girls, too. I didn't seduce them, I didn't take them for a ride, I did not abandon them, but I liked them, I desired them. I have been young too, Miguel. Forgive me. Forgive this rough old soldier. I am no man of the court; I am not versed in courtly language. Good heavens! We have had a hard life! You must not be angry with me! You must forgive me. You are handsome, Miguel, you have a high brow, and bold eyes. Give me your hand. Come on, give me your hand.

A short silence. He considers Don Miguel's hand.

It is a noble hand. The fingers are slender, the veins are light blue, a light blue that is so hard to find these days. And you are like your father.

Long silence.

Listen, Miguel. In Seville, our good old town is a modest and very ancient house, not far from the church of Caridad. The house belongs to a very old gentleman. Your father knew him. I am his friend from childhood. His name is Carillo de Mendoza. He is sick and a widower for four or five years.

Short silence.

This Carillo de Mendoza, my dear son, has only a daughter to console him in his suffering. The name of this girl, his only daughter, is Girolama. It is your mother's name, Miguel. So, this girl's name is Girolama Carillo de Mendoza. She is a noble girl. She is very nice, good and beautiful. She is just out of her childhood. You are thirty, Miguel. Oh, if only I were thirty! But you are the son of my friend and I forgive your being thirty. You never go to church, you rascal? You will go to church next week, Miguel. We'll meet there, if you like. Come, son, come. It is at the church of Caridad.

Don Fernando walks out. Silence. Almost every guest has left the banquet hall. Some have fallen asleep in the armchairs or under the table. There are some short candle stumps dying out; one can feel dawn is approaching. A Shadow pulls aside a curtain and appears to Don Miguel.

THE SHADOW

Blessed is the man whose heart is like a tombstone under the snow, and whose hope is like the name of a father inscribed on the tombstone.

Blessed is the man whose belly is the place where the cross is planted, and whose blood is like the fear of the dumb.

Blessed is the man who is cursed by his blind mother. She lifts her stick under the moon. The heart of silence is slashed to pieces.

Blessed is the man whose tears are the rains of the ruined gravestones, and whose skin is the noise of the snake among the leaves.

Blessed is the man whose son is begotten by the lust of the enemy! His son follows him in the silence of the snow, hiding behind the trees, and the cold moon looks on.

But woe, woe to the conscious man who, blind to God's beauty, prefers the emptiness of boredom to the torment of passion!

DON MIGUEL

Who are you Spirit?

THE SHADOW

I am the shadow of your past life.

SECOND FLASH

*Garden of Seville in front of the house of Carillo de
Mendoza.*

GIROLAMA CARILLO

I was not yet twelve, Miguel, when she died. It will be
four years around St. John's Day in December. It is so
good to die like that, with a pure heart and a clear mind;
it is so good that at times I reproach myself for having
cried so much. But then I was only a weak child. Certainly
my little orphan tears did not offend God because we are
very young at twelve. I know girls of that age who are still
children. Afterwards I reflected so much. My father was
already sick. You have known Don Clemente Carillo only
a short time, but you have already been able to see that
he is a bit moody. Sometimes he is harsh because of such
a long sickness. It is a terrible thing to be condemned to
immobility. Especially for a gentleman accustomed to the
life of arms.

DON MIGUEL

And how come, Girolama, I have never met any young
girls of your age in this silent house? You seem to lead a
very sad life, Girolama!

GIROLAMA

I have no friends of my own age, Don Miguel. To tell the
truth, I easily do without the company of girls of my own

age. You see I don't like either the way they laugh or the way they cry. And sometimes they talk among themselves about men in a way I don't like to hear; talk about men and the love of men. Yes, we lead a very retired life. In winter, I don't leave the house except to go to church; but in summer we spend Sundays in the country. It is one hour from Seville. We have a house there with a big, big, garden, and I love flowers very, very, much.

DON MIGUEL

You love flowers, Girolama? But I don't see them in your hair or on your person.

GIROLAMA

It is because I love flowers that I do not like girls who adorn themselves with them, as with silk or lace or colourful feathers. I never put flowers in my hair its beautiful enough, thank God! Flowers are beautiful living beings that we must let live and breathe the air of the sun and of the moon. I never pick flowers. We can very well love, in this world where we are, without wanting immediately to kill the one we love, or to imprison it behind glass, or, as people do with birds, to lock them up in a cage in which water no longer tastes like water and summer seeds no longer taste like seeds.

DON MIGUEL

So, everything is honey, and dew, and balm of sweetness in you, Girolama? Is there no dark corner in your heart? Do you never get angry?

GIROLAMA

But yes, yes! And even against these flowers, I like so much, because their Latin names are so hard to remember. They have earned me an infinite number of lectures from our abbot, who, instead of contenting himself with being good at geometry, dedicates himself to botany, too, to my great misfortune.

You were telling me a while ago that my life was sad; I don't agree at all. There is the house, the garden, the daily lesson, and the poor. There are many, a great many poor people in Seville. I have no time to get bored. And then there are books. You see, I am the one who reads to my father. I know almost all our poets, and recently we acquired "The Adventures of the Illustrious Knight of La Mancha." My father and the abbot laughed a lot, and I wanted to cry. How beautiful are the books that make you laugh and cry at the same time!

But maybe I am stretching your patience too long, Don Miguel, and you must be judging me very dull and garrulous. You look a bit surprised at seeing me so happy. Do not reproach me for this peace of mind and heart, for I neglect none of my duties.

DON MIGUEL

I was the one, Girolama, who asked you to tell me the story of your dear life. Oh, sweet life, oh beautiful and sad flower! Do not withdraw your hand; leave it here on my heart. Let the beating of my heart manage to tell you what I don't dare entrust to my voice. I've so many things to tell you! I am so changed from the day we met!

It was at the church of Caridad, remember? Around Palm Sunday, before I left for Madrid; and that same evening Don Fernando, your father's old friend, pushed me by the shoulders into this house which I feared, because you knew my life. You knew of my life, as much as can be revealed to a young girl, and it is a lot, I'm afraid. It is too much, Girolama.

GIROLAMA

I spoke to Don Fernando. Maybe I should not confess these things to you, but I spoke to Don Fernando about you. I'm no longer a child and I think that nothing is better than beautiful honesty. And Don Fernando spoke to me about you. You know how he is, our old friend Don Fernando: a bit of a teaser, but a good fellow. He told me a joke (he knew me as a baby), then suddenly he changed his tone, and even his expression. And he spoke to me about you.

DON MIGUEL

Alas, Girolama! There is no remedy to this sadness of the heart! What's done is done. Because life is like that. What's done is done.

GIROLAMA

I don't agree in the least. I see nothing so terrible in this. I know you are a bad lot, who has made many ladies cry, and beautiful ones, too. But all these women knew they were doing wrong in loving you, and even in allowing you to love them. For you have given none of them the oath, the great oath that binds for eternity, Don Miguel. You had given none of them the ring, the ring that unites soul to soul forever, Don Miguel. Ah, they knew very well what they were doing, all of them, yes, all of them!

DON MIGUEL

Silence! Your voice frightens me, Girolama! It is as if a summer-beam suddenly penetrates a place protected by the wings of night, full of crawling shapes. A night full of things dreamt of by the sickness of darkness. One day I saw a Sister of Mercy pushing her way all alone into the cell of those condemned to death. This is how your voice advances, Girolama, into my evil heart.

GIROLAMA

It is because you take me for a stupid little girl; it is because you don't know me well, Don Miguel. And it is because I am small and weak. I am sure you feel a great compassion for me, fearing you could break my wing or my little paw. But I give you leave to speak to me freely. I am not afraid of you.

Something in my heart tells me I'm your sister. I am not afraid of your eyes. No, Miguel, your look does not frighten me. I know well that at times, you are watching me as one watches a small animal he wants to catch, and it always makes me laugh when I think of it. You say woman is weak; all men say it, I think, for my father says it, and the abbot, and Don Fernando. And books say so, too. It's a fact, woman is weak. But like the bird in the air and the small mouse in the field: just wanting to catch it does not mean it is caught. And women know very well what they are doing. Wake up, Don Miguel. Women don't let themselves be taken except when God is no longer in their heart, and then it's no longer worthwhile taking them. I know well what I say and do, otherwise, would I have come here, alone? I took great interest in letting you know me, Don Miguel. For you, I know you. Three months have passed since the day we met at Caridad, Don Miguel; and you certainly are not now what you were then.

DON MIGUEL

Yes, Girolama, what you say is true; I am not what I was. I see better; yet I was not blind. Perhaps it was the light that was missing. The exterior light is a small thing; it is not the one that enlightens our life. You have lit a lamp in my heart. Here I am, like the sick man who falls asleep in darkness with the embers of fever on his forehead and the ice of desertion in his heart. A sick man who suddenly wakes up in a beautiful room in which everything is immersed in the discreet music of light; and he sees the friend he has mourned for many years…the friend who is full of happy noises to feast the man who was saved from the flood of darkness! Behold what a place of peace you've changed my heart into, Girolama! My sweetest sister! For, a while ago you said you were my sister, didn't you?

GIROLAMA

You are the man saved from the flood of darkness! You are weak, pale, and still stupefied; it is well and necessary that a sister should think for you, speak for you, support you on the way, and pray to God for you. Aren't you the man saved from the bitter water? Then, certainly, I am your sister.

DON MIGUEL

But if you truly are my sweet sister, Girolama, precisely my... No, I cannot say it, my voice is no longer my voice, my heart is no longer my heart, my life is no longer my life... Girolama, give me your weak hand, your dearest hand of a friend, of a sister, of a holy spouse!

GIROLAMA

Are you talking to a young girl or to a woman? Beware, for heaven is listening, Don Miguel.

DON MIGUEL

I am talking to a woman under the shining sky of my joy, under the heavens suspended above our heads like a perfumed vault. I am talking to you, Girolama! You who are very great, so very great as to make me afraid? What have I done with my life? What have I done with my heart? Why didn't I learn earlier that I have a good soul? Will you forgive me?

GIROLAMA

I will have to forgive you. Get up.

DON MIGUEL

What about your hand?

GIROLAMA

I will have to give it to you.

DON MIGUEL

What about your heart? Are you going to refuse it to my joy? Tell me, what about your heart?

GIROLAMA

My heart is no longer mine.

DON MIGUEL

And your great purity, and your own holiness, will you entrust them to me, for as long as time, for as long as life lasts?

GIROLAMA

For as long as eternity.

DON MIGUEL

And do you love me? Do you love me with a devoted love before men, before men?

GIROLAMA

Before God.

THIRD FLASH

Three months later. A room in Don Miguel Mañara's palace at Seville. Girolama Carillo lies on a narrow, white bed without flowers. Four candles burn, immobile. Don Miguel is crouched in a dark corner of the room. The Spirits of the Earth are within.

FIRST SPIRIT

Her eyelids are tightly closed, her jaws are firmly locked. Her arms are crossed on her breast and her hands are joined around a small wooden cross, as hard as bone. Her head rests on a pillow, neither too high nor too low. The robe does not show any crease; the robe is a perfect fit. The feet touch each other lightly. I am satisfied with my work.

SECOND SPIRIT

They have brought the coffin; I have seen it. It is of pure silver, but two strong men can lift it easily, because it is practically the coffin of a child.

THIRD SPIRIT

They have opened the old crypt of Vincentelo de Lecas. It's in perfect order. Two or three bricks to be replaced, two strokes of a trowel, and everything is in place.

FIRST SPIRIT

Tomorrow towards midday, brothers, we must go to the house of old Carillo Mendoza. When he heard of the death of his only daughter, the poor man fell into the arms of his old friend Don Fernando without a cry or a tear; after which he never opened his mouth again. Tomorrow is the third day.

DON MIGUEL

Good people! Don't make this noise of words, I pray. Do what you need to do in silence, please. I do not reproach you men for your work, but stop discussing my dear one among yourselves. I know she is dead, but I do not want people to speak of her as a dead person.

FIRST SPIRIT

He takes us for men, like he is, made out of clay and tears. And it is his great love that reads like this into the closed book of thoughts.

SECOND SPIRIT

His sad thoughts are like voices of unknown men in a dark and frozen house.

THIRD SPIRIT

There is no need to pity him. Man belongs to the earth. He must worship the Spirit of the Earth.

Speaking to Don Miguel.

Man of clay, tears have drowned your miserable brain. Words without salt drop on your mouth like lukewarm water. Wake up, look! You are alone.

DON MIGUEL

If it is my madness that speaks, if it is truly the voice of my madness that I hear, thanks be to you, O Lord my God. Let Madness take my head on her knees and sing in my ear: my little one, my little one! I do not want to be cradled by a girl. The arms of girls are as cold as death. And do not tell her, my friends that I am weeping: this would tear her poor heart to pieces.

THIRD SPIRIT

Get up, speak, act, and weep like a man. Aren't you a man, Mañara? Aren't you a son of Sorrow?

Get up; the mourning clothes are ready. You must walk up to the grave with a dignified air. And watch out for the mud on the road, for it is already autumn. Three months have elapsed since the summer day of your wedding. You must not overlook the calculation of the months and the days, son of the Earth.

DON MIGUEL

I will follow the coffin as a small child that is led to the church; and I will do all that they'll tell me to do. I am a poor unhappy man. I do not want people to get angry because of me. And I will not go and hang myself among the willows by the riverside. I will do nothing that God forbids. God has created me, and I will have to go on living.

THIRD SPIRIT

Think of the Earth, son of Sorrow. All the rest is worth nothing. You have a heart for hope, and hands for work. You need to go on living, and to live long, and to say with men: "It is a joy for me." And when your arms are broken, and when your old bones are painful, you will get up earlier than usual. When your white hair is like the disease of the tree, one day you will get up earlier than usual, and you will light the frail lamp in the grey hour. Then you'll set your hand to work for the last time.

FIRST SPIRIT

But on the threshold like a branch without bark you'll fall. Then the big cold bed will be opened.

SECOND SPIRIT

And the coffin will be brought.

THIRD SPIRIT

And the Vincentelo de Lecas' crypt will be opened.

THE THREE SPIRITS

But till that beautiful day you must live, son of Earth.

The Spirits go away. A long silence. The hours are heard to strike.

DON MIGUEL

Sorrow, Sorrow, why did you beget me? Why did you not crash my head between two innocent stones, more kind than the breasts of your love?

You tell me, Sorrow, that you are my mother. But if you are, you must know what hell cries here, mother, in this old heart. Is it for this you lulled me in the winter nights, in the light of fireplaces, where orphaned time cried out? Tell me: is it for this that you lulled me with tears and dreams in your sad eyes, in your dear eyes the colour of journey and of wind? You laid me in a cradle: would that you had thrown me in to a grave! You kissed my body from the small feet to the poor head: why weren't you like the beasts in the woods, who choke their cubs to death? O mother!

Cursed be your sweetness, you who gave me birth in Sorrow! Cursed be your belly, cursed be your womb, you who gave me this sad body, this lonely heart.

And yet you are not the sister of the she-wolf who gives birth hungry in the light of a sad moon like a face kissed by the plague. We must leave tenderness to the females in the woods, whose skin tastes of hunger. Aren't you the daughter of men, O Sorrow?

Mother, mother! I have lost everything, my life is widowed, my lust weeps and I am the father of fright, of folly, and of death. O Sorrow, my mother, what did you make of me?

THE SPIRIT OF HEAVEN

Mañara, Mañara!

DON MIGUEL

Who is calling me? I know this voice. Where did I hear it before, and when? It is as if the echo of the birth-cry should be awakened suddenly in an old man's heart.

THE SPIRIT OF HEAVEN

Mañara, Mañara! Beloved son!

DON MIGUEL

It is like the ghost of a sweet sun on the water. It is like the steamy breeze of the apple tree.

THE SPIRIT OF HEAVEN

Mañara, Mañara! Rejoice!

DON MIGUEL

I do not understand you. Speak more clearly.

THE SPIRIT OF HEAVEN

Open your ear.

*A short silence. Under the windows a procession passes
by.*

SONG

The sweat of death runs in his eyes. He walks under the
cross towards his last day. What thing of beauty is there
here to be seen? Tell us, Son of Man!

The water of this country is like the eye of the blind man.
The stone of this country is like the heart of the King. The
tree of this country is a torture pole for you, Love, son of
Heavens.

He has broken the bread; he has poured the wine.

This is the flesh; this is the blood.

Let he who has ears hear!

He prayed and got up. His beloved ones were lying under
the olive tree.

Simon, are you asleep?

He cried and he got up. His dear children were dreaming
under the olive tree. You can sleep now, says the Son of
Man. They came with swords and lanterns: "I greet you,
Master." The brother has kissed the brother on the cheek.
The right ear was cut, and see, it is healed so that man may
understand.

The cock has crowed twice. There is no love left; all is
forgotten.

The cock has crowed in the loneliness of your heart, Son of Man.

The crown is on your head; the reed is in your hand. The face is blind to the spit and the blood.

Hail, king of the Jews.

The clothes have been divided. The thieves are dead.

"I thirst," the heart of life cries out.

But the sponge has fallen back and the side is pierced and all is accomplished.

Now we know that he is the Son of the living God and that he is with us till the end of the world. Amen.

DON MIGUEL

Amen.

FOURTH FLASH

Parlour in the Convent of Caridad, Seville.

DON MIGUEL

Father, I am here asking for asylum. And for protection.

THE ABBOT

And against whom, my son?

DON MIGUEL

Against myself.

THE ABBOT

Who are you then?

DON MIGUEL

Mañara.

> *The Abbot takes one step back.*

THE ABBOT

Your place is not here. You have the smell of burning about you.

DON MIGUEL

It is the Eternal love that consumes me, Father.

He throws himself on his knees.

THE ABBOT

And what do you come here seeking, my son?

DON MIGUEL

The punishment of the jealous God. Humility of heart. Love for reality.

THE ABBOT

You talk like a poor sinner. Get up. I know your crimes, Don Miguel de Leca; but it is necessary that the black confession pour from your mouth like the ugliness of vomit. The repentance of the heart is nothing if it doesn't climb all the way up to the teeth and flood the lips with bitterness. If you are God's friend, then, speak. And it is necessary that the Truth be naked, without any veil of shame or sorrow. Say: "I did this, I that." Speak.

DON MIGUEL

I did not work the six days. I have done no work at all. And on the seventh day, my work was to blaspheme, to spit on the earth and on God. I honoured neither father nor mother. My father cursed me, my mother died of sorrow.

I lied. A thousand times, I said: "I love" while my heart was laughing a wicked laughter. And a liar can take back what he has said but I, how could I take back what I have said?

I stole. I stole innocence. But the penitent gives back, and I, I cannot give back.

I killed. And my victims are black with my sin before the face of God and filthy with their lust, and my own. I have desired the house of my neighbour; I even set the house of my neighbour on the fire with my desire. And it is a house that one cannot rebuild with money. I did all this. I did all this, Father.

Silence.

And then a woman stood up in the bend of a bad road. She was calm like the dream of water, beautiful like the light of honey, innocent like the laughter of small children. She talked to me of God, and taught me to pray. At night, I repeated the words of her prayer, like a child. The woman's name is Girolama, Father. Girolama Carillo Mendoza is the name of my wife, Father.

THE ABBOT

The love of this woman, of this Girolama, was a very good thing. Why then are you here, and all tears, Don Miguel Mañara?

DON MIGUEL

This woman, all sweet and all mine, this Girolama, Father, is dead.

THE ABBOT

Come on. Weep if you need to, but do not make all this noise.

He prays for a moment, then he lifts up his face.

DON MIGUEL

I haven't told you everything, Father.

THE ABBOT

One must not talk again of these poor things, of these stupid things, my grown-up child. Do you understand? These are stories to be left to those whom the great pride of the small sins still torments.

But you Miguel, my great villain, beloved son, what could you have to tell me? Who does not know the great Mañara? For a long time I've been watching you. We see everything here, despite our eyes on the breviary. Listen to me. I've let you cry on my lap, and you cried like a newborn. And now I lift my finger, and see how full of anger I am! Listen to how I shout: "Silence!" What do you know of your sorrow, my son? You came here to be reproached and scolded, and now you are reproaching Penance for its sweet voice. They are all the same; they are terrible, these children. Since the lord is sweet, they would like to stuff themselves until they burst. You had come out of your house as if you were going to buy fruit. You have come. You are here. And all is well.

DON MIGUEL

I am afraid of your great compassion, Father. I feel so
wrapped up; embraced by kindness. You must not be so
sweet, Father. I feel I'm melted by your dear tenderness. I
am ashamed. Nobody has ever spoken to me like this.

THE ABBOT

But yes. But yes.

You have been much loved, and you know it very well,
you rascal, because they talked sweetly to you many, many
times. Are you going to be ungrateful? No. You say so
because you are dressed in vanity, and because your hair is
clean and well combed. You wear a beautiful jacket; thank
God I am not a young girl! Your white hands have clean
and well-cared-for fingers. You would like, I bet, to be
already dressed in rags, waving around a long grey beard
still with dirt and heavy with rain! I know you are ready to
let the smelly cobblestones resound with your penitent's
bowl, my graceful dandy.

Come on, come on! Do not cry, my son. No! He does not
want to smile, my begging monk. I cannot get a smile out
of him! Don't you understand then, my son? The fact is
you are thinking of things that are no more and that never
were, my son.

But is it necessary to remind you that you have come, that
you are here, that all is well? What is there in that head of
his, Lord?

DON MIGUEL

How can you read my heart in this way, Father? You did not even give me time to open it all to you. How do you read my heart, a closed book, like this, Father?

THE ABBOT

Get up. You are being strange. And stop embracing my knees. Can't you keep quiet? I'll have your cell prepared. Do you hear me? I want to have you very close. Your nights will be very long, deserted, and hard. Just wait a bit and see what comes to a man dressed in vanity! You are going to find out what prayer is all about. You are going to know how a man prays, alone, at night, between four walls made of eternity. Ah, prayer is not your fountains of tears under the moon! Say your prayers among four walls that pretend to be deaf. Speak your litanies virgin of thought and naked of reason as long as a shadow of love escapes. I want to have you very close. But you will never call for me. Understand? You will only say to yourself, "the Father is there, behind these walls that never dream. The Father is there, he is old, and he sleeps on his three planks. And I am all alone with the heart of stone, and I breathe my prayers into the ear of stone." For you men dressed in colors say that walls have ears for your plots and your blasphemies. But here, life is a thing very different from a smile in a woman's lipstick or a tear fallen on glass. Here the stones are full of a patience that waits and a waiting that listens.

DON MIGUEL

Dark cell! Image of my heart! Lovable mortifications! Silence of catacombs! How I love you already!

THE ABBOT

Love and haste do not agree, Mañara. It is by patience that love is measured. This is the pace of love: a pace both regular and sure. The pace of love that walks between two jasmine hedges, arm in arm with a girl, or alone between two rows of tombs. Patience. You have not come here, sir, to be tortured. Life is long here. Infancy and education are necessary, along with youth, and teaching. Only then will you develop a maturity curious about the true weight of things, and a slow old age in love with the grave. With what prudence must we move then! For the burning hair-shirt has no love for the violence that quenches the blood's itching. So, you must keep very still in a short, narrow coffin when you desire to sleep an hour or two. For in prayer, sleep is as empty and as deep as the instant.

To let your own blood is something sweetly fiendish; and sleeplessness consumes the heart. Now, life is long here, you understand. And too exasperated a hunger is a temptation. You must chew the foul grass and the lukewarm root like an animal which has before it beautiful meadows and long, long hours of summer.

And you must talk to Eternity with precious and clear syllables even at night, when its love grabs you by the throat like a murderer.

Know too that it is an excellent thing to remain faithful to the word that was ordered, a dam of granite for the bitter waters of your love! For it is necessary that prayer be a fast before it is a banquet, and nakedness of heart before it is a mantle of heaven buzzing with worlds. Perhaps a day will come when God allows you to enter brutally, like an axe, into the flesh of the tree. A day will come when you fall madly like a stone into the night of the water, and to slip, singing like fire, into the heart of metal. And on that day you will know of what flesh the world is made. You will speak freely to the soul of the world, the soul of the tree, of the soul of the water, and of the metal; and you will speak to it with the voice of the wind and of the rain and of a woman in love.

My son! Man has cried numberless times, not prostrated, but standing up straight before God, breathing his love onto him full in His face, like a fire in a forest or in a great city. And the Lord laughed, because the angels were afraid. My dear child, all this may well come one day, when the snake has changed his skin. But one must start from the beginning: this is essential.

To bite the stone and to bark, "Lord, Lord, Lord!" is to weep and serve a heartless woman. You must leave this to the betrayed who sigh for one night, six months, or ten years.

Life is long here.

You will beware therefore of inventing prayers. You will sing humbly with the book of the poor in spirit. And you will wait.

From the last nightly spark of your madness, the first dawn will spring up!

The crater of the heart cries and thunders and the black vomit will leave the cloud, falling back in grey famine on the field and the vineyard. A prayer that devastates passion is like that. But when the heart has fallen asleep in the balm of the years, when the flesh has died and the blood has gone pale, you will no longer speak to God of yourself. When the marrow has gone dry, and when love and sorrow are past, you will no longer speak to God of yourself. When love, sorrow, and hatred have become ghosts that the sword penetrates as it does water, and when the lip hits nothing more than its own wound, as in molten glass, it is then that you speak to God no longer of yourself and of your own miserable unhappiness, but of man. It is then you will speak to God of the breaking waves of sea foam, of the sand, of the wind, and of the rain! Do you know which saint said, "Behold brother wind and sister rain?"

O my son, if you knew what things man can tell God when man's flesh becomes a cry; a cry of God worshiping Himself!

You do not have the face of a man who is listening, Miguel. You are thinking too much of your own sorrow. Why do you seek sorrow? Why are you afraid of losing what has managed to find you? Penance is not sorrow. It is love.

DON MIGUEL

I hear you Father. It is not in me to drown my shame in the rapture of my sorrow! Let God's hands measure the bitter dosage of day and night, not mine! No, the beautiful innocent sky will not say, "Here is Mañara, bringing me a sorrow daubed in colours that he worships like the skin of a crying prostitute!" No, Father. You will have in me a docile animal to turn your mill, an ox that will allow its neck and flanks to be anointed with that pity that heals the

75

sting of the goad and puts to sleep for the night the burn of the whip. So that dawn may find us strong! And as happy as the merry crow of the cock! And full of a vigour hungry for expiation!

THE ABBOT

God's goodness! He is already chatting, my Mañara, like a monk begging for his poor amidst a laughing colourful crowd, at noon on Sunday when the Christian sun resounds, when the whole town tastes of a Mass that was too long, and of Sunday lunch. Eh, slow down, sir. Spare your eloquence and fire for the autumn day and the winter night, when, barefoot, dirty, and dressed in the odour of years, you will rattle your bowl. Under the window of the bigot, at the door of the old greedy merchant, or in the hallway of the prostitute that is so generous as to make you cry, you will need to rattle your bowl. Eh, take your time, sir, take your time. We aren't there yet, are we? I look and see, may heaven forgive me, not the mangy donkey with a hollow back, loaded with the week's bread, but rather a battle-horse. I see not the donkey from the mill that comes to eat from the hand of the friar doorkeeper, but rather a battle-horse well-fed with barley, washed in Mauritanian sand, and spurred by the Pagan. What a flame! What a frightening impatience! Take it easy! Take it easy, my dear son! And with a little goodwill everything will work out. I go at once to give the necessary orders.

He goes out.

DON MIGUEL

Look at the moon! Look at the earth! Look at man so weak and at his great sorrow. And yet, despite all these things that are, I dare not say that You are.

Who am I, then, that I should dare say that You are? I am not sure. I have no right to be sure of anything apart from one: of my love, of my love, of my blind love for You. Nothing is pure, except my love for You. Nothing is great, except my love for You. The dream has vanished. The passion has run away. The remembrance was canceled. Love has remained. Nothing is sincere, except my love for You. Nothing is real, except my love for You. Nothing is immortal, except my love for You.

For I am nothing but one dead man among the dead whom I have loved, I am nothing but a name that fills the mouth of the living with sand. What's left is Love. Ah, Beauty! The sad, poor Beauty! But I want to praise Beauty, for it is from Beauty that Sorrow is born. The beloved of the Beloved. Your great love burns my heart. Your great love is my sole certainty. O tears! O hunger for eternity! O joy! Alas! Forgive! Alas! Love me!

FIFTH FLASH

In front of the church of Caridad, Seville. An exuberant
Sunday crowd. Two religious men of the Order of
Caridad are in the forefront.

FIRST RELIGIOUS MAN

So, then, what do you think, brother? As for me, I am still like
the leaves of the aspen. That so simple a language should
fill your head and your heart with heaven is something,
in truth, that surpasses our way of understanding. I had to
make a big effort, especially towards the end of the speech,
to hold back my tears; and at the bottom of my throat, I
still have a choked cough that stings like the nettle. What
a holy man is friar Miguel of God! And what a skillful
orator! I want to wait here for our reverend Father and
ask him what effect such a beautiful language can have on
the heart of God. I have not studied and I read only with
difficulty what is in the books. The spade and rake are
my usual companions. If a word that's just a bit difficult
comes poking my ear, there I am as mute as our friend the
earthworm. Today, instead, I understood everything; the
good word of the penitent has fallen into my heart like
a handful of precious seed. And do you know that at the
beginning of the sermon I had to close my eyes and bite
my lip so as not to laugh? Is this the way to speak of our
Lord? I thought: "Here is a mule-driver's or a spinster's

language; and are we children to hear such things said to us?" And then, suddenly, I perceived that the voice did not come from a man's mouth, but as if from the lips of a deep wound. And when he spoke to us of the Lord who walked on the sea, his eloquence became as sweet to my ear as the voice of great waters suddenly calm and penetrated by a light of tenderness.

SECOND RELIGIOUS MAN

I have followed that singular speech like you, Brother, in all its points. I liked its movement and colour, but see, I have become yellow among the parchments, and my old head is that of a librarian. Alas! Men are strange creatures!

Certainly, frank speaking can be enthralling, but speaking too frankly often touches on heresy. Being carried away by passion, agreeable as it may seem, will never equal, in my opinion, a well-pondered order.

FIRST RELIGIOUS MAN

It's not for me, surely, to contradict you, Brother; the most boring preachers know less than you do. Grant, anyway, that the word was edifying, and that, as it came from the heart, it found the way into the heart. Consider Mañara's life too, his horrible past, and his ardent repentance. He has this love for the poor that stings him like a fire, and makes him run around from early morning, as dirty as a pig, his beard in the wind, hunger and thirst in his mouth, a bowl in his hand. Mañara has this terrible humility that hits his knees like a stone twenty times a day, and throws him down, all in tears, at the feet of a beggar who teases him and on the hard road of the prostitute. This funny tenderness for the little ones wins for our madman, from charmed mothers, caresses like one gives to a donkey or to a cow. I too find myself at times speaking to him too sweetly, as when you discover you have destroyed the den of some small animal in the garden with the stroke of a spade. Consider again this bitter gratitude that for him makes all this earth of sorrow and sins a host sweet to his saliva; a comfortable kneeler. Didn't I surprise him, one day, prostrated in a field, while he talked to the deaf clay as to his mother? And it was a Sunday last month when I saw him run to a stone a drunkard had thrown at him, pick it up, and kiss it ever so tenderly.

But here he comes out of the church, surrounded by beggars. See how he talks, red-checked and breathless, with the Reverend Abbot who smiles back at him. I never saw him so joyful and childlike.

SECOND RELIGIOUS MAN

What is this?

The paralytic beggar Johannes Mendelez, all numb and stiff, pitifully drags himself out of the church. Laughter and cries welcome him into the square.

A MAN'S VOICE

Look at our crippled stoup-kisser, Johannes Mendelez! That old thief who was struck by God's anger. Come here, come here everybody! We are allowed to laugh a bit after those long litanies.

A CHILD'S VOICE

Today I throw this stone into his teeth. Yesterday my dog bit him, and he called me with an affectionate voice, certainly to beat me.

The stone hits Johannes full in the chest,
and he falls with a cry.

DON MIGUEL

Lord, they have hit a poor sick old man! I see the faces of men and Christians lit up with pleasure, as if the juggler had unfolded his carpet.

A WOMAN'S VOICE

It is Johannes Mendelez, the crippled, old, crow thief whom a child has hit with a stone, my good monk. It is only Johannes, the gallows-pendant, who was released last winter, after fourteen years in the galleys. It'd be better to kill him, like the old dog he is. When a bone is thrown to him, he starts praying, to tease us, and then he comes back at sunset to steal the dog's soup from honest people.

DON MIGUEL

Johannes, Johannes, do you hear me?

JOHANNES

You are the holy monk Mañara. I recognize your voice. It is a sweet voice.

DON MIGUEL

Johannes, place your soul in God's hands. You look like someone who is going to die.

JOHANNES

Alas, no! The hour has not come yet. Don't you worry, good monk. Alas, no. Despite my old age, my weakness, and my pain, God refuses me my sleep. I'll have to live days and days, nights and nights, crawling like a worm, screeching like an axle that has not been oiled, and fighting over the marrow-less bone with a stray dog. The moment has not come. Expiation is long, my good monk.

DON MIGUEL

Expiation is very long, Johannes, but it is also very sweet. You do not speak like an enemy of God.

JOHANNES

For a very long time I was an enemy of God, like my father the bandit, and my mother the street-girl. My sad mother did not have the courage to strangle me, instead she fed me with her thief's milk on her prostitute's bed. I was eight years old when a fornicating priest, moved to pity, spoke to me of the Father, of the Son, and of the Spirit. Seeing I was weeping, the priest also wept bitterly. It was he who taught me to pray, and I've prayed for him, the bad priest, and for my miserable mother. And when the sweet time for love came, my heart fell in love with a young gypsy, wild like me, and rejected like me. She loved me, and her people chased her away like a bitch, because of her love for a Christian bastard. The days were hard, good monk. Then I stole, to feed her sweet woman's mouth. The life of the galleys slowly ate away my bones. When my leg was drenched like a rag under the rain they threw me ashore with a pair of crutches, and I came here to die, where God had me born.

DON MIGUEL

Lord, Lord, I call you from Capernaum.
Lord, Lord, I lift my voice from the land of the Gadarenes.

Lord, Lord, I think of you at the borders of Tyre and Sidon.

Lord, Lord, my voice reaches you from the villages of Decapolis.
Lord, Lord, I shout to you from Bethsaida.
Lord, Lord, come to my aid at the borders of Judaea beyond the Jordan.
Amen.

To the paralytic.

You have suffered much from men, Johannes, my brother. And what name do you give God, in your thoughts? Do you call Him Sorrow, or Justice, or Vengeance?

JOHANNES

I call him by the name which is his, friar Mañara; that same name that you have shouted a while ago from the pulpit, good friar Mañara.

DON MIGUEL

And what is it?

JOHANNES

Love.

DON MIGUEL

Throw away your crutches.

After a moment of hesitation, Johannes throws away his crutches.

DON MIGUEL

Get up and walk.

Johannes Mendelez gets up and without looking at anyone goes back towards the church shouting in a terrible voice: "Hosanna! Hosanna!" The abbot of the Caridad and his monks kiss the dress of Don Miguel Mañara. The people shout: "Miracle!" Then they throw themselves to their knees imploring the blessing of the Penitent.

SIXTH FLASH

A courtyard in the convent of Caridad. The silence of the last moments of night. The sky is full of stars, and yet it seems that day is already here. A small door opens noiselessly. Miguel Mañara *appears, a lantern in his hand and a bag on his shoulder. He is very old, his hair is white, and his hands tremble. He leans on a stick.*

DON MIGUEL

O my heart! O my child! You did not sleep, and here is the day. Here is the day; it arrives and it is astonished at finding yesterday's moon in the sky. Here are you alone under the cold tears of a night lost forever, alone with your thoughts of yesterday, like the mowed grass. O face in tears! O severe Eternity!

Silence.

They are dead. Unknown sleepers surround me. Those whom my heart loved have been dead a long time. Only one saw me growing old: the friar gardener, the one who knows the thought of the herbs and the intentions of the air. All the others are dead. O morning moon! O sad look of Eternity.

Silence.

Not everything has been said; not everything has been done. One has to pray; one has to act. The immense heart of anguish is like the noise of the wing that is broken on water. The whole night, the whole night! Anguish was at my side like a wife who loves and whom for a long time one has stopped loving.

Silence.

I got up early and I have joined these strong hands in the glow of the lantern. I have much to do today, and my heart is right in loving the weak lamp of the morning and the mechanical prayer in the empty blue cold, which does not fall from the moon and is not the breath of the morning.

Silence.

O morning moon! How you have the face of those who see strange and profound things! The hungry man bites his own breath and eats it, and falls asleep in the water of his own weakness. The sick worker collects his tools coughing. The abandoned girl recognizes with fright the garret, the splinter of mirror and the broom. She blankly watches her barren womb, and suddenly thinks of the shrieking of the well.

Silence.

Lord! Lord, give us our daily hope! O Father, O Son, give us our daily courage! As the leper beggar, with his back stuck to the wall stretches his bowl towards the soup, so will I stretch my young heart towards the perfumed warmth of the amorous life!

Give me my daily share of love, and measure it out generously, because of the others who need it. With this love may I go, overflowing, towards those who do not love you and insult me. With this love may I say: "This is

His liberality." For these are not the gifts of His heart, but only the crumbs swept away from His table. Here is what remains in the bowl of the unworthy and surfeited servant.

O road! O city! O kingdom! O earth! Come and eat! For thus is the Most High, for He is the Lord Love! I am Mañara, the one who lies when he says: "I love." And because I said to the Eternal that I loved Him, my heart is joyful and my hands are as desirable as bread.

What does Paul, the scoundrel, say? And what does Mary, the prostitute, say? They say, "That which was stolen and lost was stolen and lost forever."

I am Mañara. And the one I love says: "These things have not been. If he has stolen, if he has killed: let these things be forgotten!" Only he is.

Silence. Dawn at the horizon.

The silence has the smell of the apple tree that dreams; the air that wears an angel's robe. The breath of the earth is like the yawning of the ox. The great wall takes the colour of the almond tree. Here is dawn. The well creaks like the lazy schoolboy. The echo gets up from its bed. Here are the water carriers. The straw of the stables shakes. The cock! The cock crows as to make man's heart weep. Here is day! O earth! O beloved!

He puts out the lantern, and then listens intently.

And I hear a bell: one, two, three, four, five! A monk's hour. And I hear the trumpet: "Tra ra! Tra ra ra!" A soldier's hour.

He goes towards the door on the street,
but suddenly on the threshold,
a form wrapped in a dark mantle stands up.

THE UNKNOWN ONE

Stop.

DON MIGUEL

I do not know this man and the door is locked. He could
not have climbed over the wall.

THE UNKNOWN ONE

You got up earlier than usual, Mañara. You have lit the
small lamp and you have been praying. And now you want
to take up your work for the last time.

DON MIGUEL

Certainly I am day dreaming. Yet I recognize the voice
and remember the words. It was a long, long time ago.
Where did I hear this? But I'm wasting my time. Come
on then, old heart, courage! And you, old legs, come on!

THE UNKNOWN ONE

Stop.

The game has gone on too long. Everything has had its
time. We shall no longer go to take bread to those children,

or that new bowl to Pablo Perez, our handsome blind fiddler. Everything has had its time, Mañara. There is a time for youth; there is a time for old age. Then comes death. Thus speaks the Spirit of the Earth.

DON MIGUEL

A veil is fluttering before my eyes, and my legs are sinking in sand. My stomach is closing, and anguish is catching in my throat.

THE SPIRIT

I am the Spirit of the Earth. Beware. You have a ghost's name on your lips. I am, I am. Truly I am, through the heart and the reason of Man. Look at me. I have put on my true form. Here is the Lord; here is the Prince of the kingdoms of the earth. Recognize me.

He opens his mantle.

DON MIGUEL

O terrible face! O sad face...

THE SPIRIT

I am the one who is. I am the heart of the earth. All the rest is vanity. As the handsome thief clasps the excited prostitute in his arms, so I hold the warm earth tight against my breast.

Listen how the earth, the girl with the wide womb, teases you, ghost-hunters; empty toys of Justice. Listen! Listen to what the great lover whispers in your hairy ear:

"What do they know of me, these gelded ones? I make them pay dearly the joy of my odour! You. You are my lover and my master! Injustice drugs your mouth, your hairy hand is warm on my head. I will bring handsome royal sons for you, who will love the mysterious gold and the vapour of blood. I will give them a forehead as low as yours, my love, and enormous hands, and large licking mouths, my love. Their faces will be warm and pale like the lightning. And from the first day they will seek their joy in the grief of little ones."

Thus, speaks the Earth to its Lord, to its Master:

"We shall make for our daughter a bed of scarlet and her two breasts will call the passer-by like the fountains of the city, like the unsealed springs. And our daughter will be as beautiful as the pomegranate broken by the weight of its own fall. And she will say with a milky stammer: 'Love cannot be a sin.' And behold! Your royal seal will be visible on her face long kissed by the fire that passes and forgets. Her tongue will then be like the head of the snake that dances and the shadow of the joyful hours will be encrusted on the dial of her face. And one day her face will be like a dance and the shadow of the joyful hours will be your mantle and you will give her children."

Thus, speaks the Earth to its Lord, to its Master:

"The sons will be clothed in iron; the daughters will shine with perfumes. And gold will resound on the tables. The wombs will offer themselves to whoever offers most. Whoever has a sweet heart and will meet my eyes will be like the frightened insect in the fold of the earth. He will look at his mother and will say: I smell betrayal, why isn't that the face of an old woman that barks at the moon? And he will be sleepy and will not dare entrust his head to his wife's breast: for adultery will have passed there. And they'll have time to laugh over it! The adulterous man dreams poisonous dreams! And the man will call on his daughter, the virgin, and glancing at her mouth he will bow his head."

Thus, speaks the Earth to its Lord, to its Master:

"And man will entrust his heritage to the worms of the ruins, to the nettle's root, in a place which his fiery-eyed brother does not visit. All mouths will be full of lies, and all hearts will secretly desire death. The strongest and greediest of our sons will be a king and the weakest and the most cunning will be a priest. They will hold hands and laugh in their beards. And on the Mount of Temptation, once a year, you will blow on the secret fire through the rumbling of the crater. Then what is supposed to swim will walk like the beast of the forest and what is supposed to crawl will fly like fire. And the vermin of the great wall will come and reveal to us the secret thought of man."

Thus speaks the Earth, to the prince of the Kingdoms of the Earth:

"Come on, Mañara, get up. You know very well that you belong to me. Did you not give me the best of yourself, the poem of your youth?"

DON MIGUEL

Lifting his hands to heaven.

I am a stranger on the earth; do not hide your commands from me.

Do not leave me alone in my distress. Come close; there is none else to help.

My soul lies in the dust; give me life according to your word.

Teach me discernment and knowledge, for I trust in your commands.

Listen, then, to my cry, for I am in the depths of distress.

Bring my soul out of this prison.

The apparition vanishes.

THE SPIRIT OF HEAVEN

Miguel! Miguel!

DON MIGUEL

Here I am.

A very long silence. A lizard comes to warm itself on a stone near the dead man.

The small door of the Convent opens slowly. Enter the friar gardener – he is the first religious man in the Fifth Flash.

He is extremely old and broken. He walks in very short steps while looking at the ground.

Reaching the corpse of Miguel, he stops, showing no surprise.

THE FRIAR GARDENER

Friar Miguel, are you sleeping?

*He touches him lightly. Silence. He recites
a short prayer and makes a large sign of the cross
embracing the four horizons.*

Now I am alone.

Now I am among the living like the naked branch whose dry noise frightens the evening wind. But my heart is joyful like the nest that remembers and like the earth that hopes under the snow. For I know that everything is where it is supposed to be and goes where it is supposed to go: to the place assigned to it by a Wisdom that, heaven be praised, is not our own

He considers at length the calm face of Miguel.

Here Magdalene, is your brother.

Here Teresa, is your brother.

TO THE PRAISE OF CHRIST. AMEN.

www.ingramcontent.com/pod-product-compliance
Lightning Source LLC
Jackson TN
JSHW011030060525
83900JS00013B/83